Pattern Aware™ Success Guide

Companion to Award Winning

'Don't Bring It to Work'

SYLVIA LAFAIR

Copyright © 2013 by Sylvia Lafair, PhD

Published June 2013

ISBN 978-0-9883625-4-3

creative energy options

CEO

PUBLISHING

45 Country Place Lane
White Haven, PA 18661
Phone (570) 636-3858
Fax (570) 6365387
Info@ceoptions.com
www.ceoptions.com

Dear Reader,

This is a daily guide to increase your self-awareness and ability to be a leading force in your workplace.

Thank you for taking this step to enhance your career and your life.

This book gives you the day to day roadmap to find the way OUT of what no longer supports your life. It is organized for you to strengthen the capacity to Observe, Understand, and Transform patterns that you no longer need nor want.

There are foundational, intermediate and advanced sections.

The way OUT of old ingrained behavior patterns is to

> *Observe*
>
> *Understand*
>
> *Transform*

We suggest you print this out and use as a journal or make your notes in your own journal so you can reference as you go through the daily exercises.

As you complete each section, you'll see changes in the way you view all your interactions. So let the games of a better life begin –enjoy your daily reflecting on becoming Pattern Aware for unlimited success!

And remember, along the way, email us at info@ceoptions.com or call 570-636-3858 with questions, concerns or comments on this companion to "Don't Bring It to Work".

We are here to support you in any way we can.

If you have not yet taken the Pattern Aware Quiz on www.sylvialafair.com, then do so now before you start. It will help you gain clarity about the patterns that are holding you back. And here's the bonus—as a purchaser of this book you are entitled to a free 1/2 hour coaching session on your quiz results.

All you have to do is take the quiz and email info@ceoptions.com and state, "I'm ready for my free coaching session." We will contact you to set it up.

Best of everything,

Sylvia Lafair

Table of Contents:

The Way OUT

Step One: Learn to OBSERVE

Pages 5 - 22

Step Two: Understand Your Patterns

Pages 25 - 43

Step Three: Time to Transform

Pages 45 - 59

Pattern Aware Resources

Pages 60- 62

From NOW to NEW

Begin by OBSERVING

Receiving knowledge of the outside world through the senses. Filter sensory information through the thought process—input received via hearing, sight, smell, taste, or touch and analyzed either through rational or irrational means.

Life is full of beauty. Notice it. Notice the bumblebee, the small child, and the smiling faces. Smell the rain, and feel the wind. Live your life to the fullest potential, and fight for your dreams.

- Ashley Smith

Learn by Observing

Day 1: STOP!!

Every hour on the hour for 4 hours take 1 minute and STOP.

Whether you are at your desk, walking down a hall, attending a meeting, become ultra-observant.

Notice:

- Your environment

  Inside: notice the walls, windows

  Outside: notice the trees, plants, sky

- Colors

- Textures

- Smells

- Sounds

What have you observed?

Hour One:

_____

_____

Hour Two:

_____

_____

Hour Three:

_____

_____

Hour Four:

_____

_____

Day 2: Observe

At least 4 times a day **STOP** and pay attention to your body:

- Standing: legs, arms, spine

- Sitting: rump, shoulders

- Lying down: abdomen, head

What are you aware of?

      Breath, tension spots, heart beating

What did you observe?

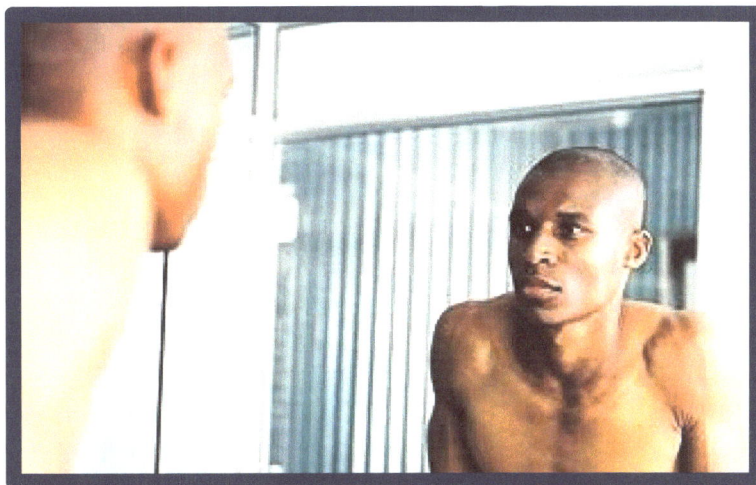

Day 3: Observe and Think

Notice how you think about the world around you.

Do you accept/judge/appreciate?

Write down 3 things you see that you usually ignore.

1. _

2. _

3. _

Pick one and take a few minutes to really look at it.

To acquire knowledge, one must study; to acquire wisdom, one must observe. - *Marilyn vos Savant*

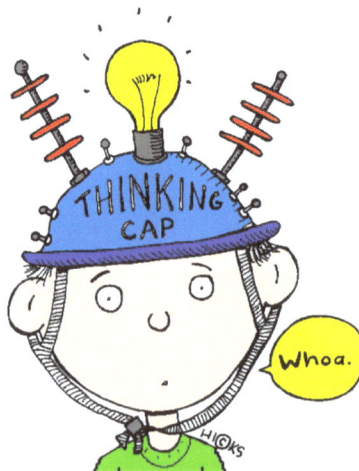

Day 4: Observe and Emote (FEEL)

From the following list of emotions **CIRCLE** the ones that best describe you. Trust your gut: some words will impact you more than others. Then, take **ONE** from the list of those circled and check off how many times that emotion shows up for you today.

Aggressive	Envious	Miserable
Aggravated	Excited	Negative
Alienated	Exhausted	Optimistic
Angry	Fearful	Paranoid
Annoyed	Frightened	Peaceful
Anxious	Frustrated	Proud
Apathetic	Guilty	Puzzled
Bashful	Happy	Regretful
Careful	Helpless	Relieved
Cautious	Hopeful	Sad
Confident	Hostile	Satisfied
Confused	Humiliated	Shocked
Curious	Hurt	Shy
Depressed	Hysterical	Sorry
Determined	Innocent	Sure
Disappointed	Interested	Surprised
Discouraged	Jealous	Suspicious
Disgusted	Lonely	Thoughtful
Ecstatic	Loved	Undecided
Embarrassed	Love Struck	Withdrawn
Enthusiastic	Mischievous	

Day 5: Observe and Write

Take 5 minutes (*you pick the time of day*) and write a short paragraph about what is happening in your environment.

Then go back and circle the words that describe how you feel.

_____

_____

_____

_____

_____

_____

_____

_____

_____

_____

_____

_____

_____

_____

_____

_____

> *To observe without evaluating is the highest form of intelligence*
>
> *- J. Krishnamurti*

> *If you observe well, your own heart will answer.*
>
> *- Rene Schwaller de Lubicz*

Day 6: Observe and Do

From the following list pick one attribute you admire and practice it with everyone you connect with today.

- Listen without comment
- Ask without judgment
- Acknowledgement
- Smile
- Feedback without blaming

Day 7: Observe Your Story

If your life were a play what would be the title?

_____

Jot down during the day when the title shows up.

_____

_____

_____

_____

_____

Day 8: Change Your Story

- Do one thing today that would make your story different—

For example: call someone you haven't talked with in a while, say thank you to someone you often ignore, or ask an opinion of someone you don't often talk with.

A quick look at the 13 most common patterns in the workplace.

The **Super Achiever** – must win at all costs

The **Rebel** – can't accept any authority

The **Procrastinator** – won't finish anything

The **Clown**– reduces everything to a joke

The **Persecutor** – bullies people into misery

The **Victim** – too scared to take any action

The **Rescuer** – demands to be the big hero

The **Drama Queen/King** – makes emotional scenes

The **Martyr** – does everyone else's work

The **Pleaser** – says what folks want to hear

The **Avoider** – dodges work and responsibility

The **Denier** – won't face problems directly

The **Splitter** – secretly sets up conflict

Day 9: Pattern Awareness

Choose from the list of patterns on page 11. Select one of the patterns —do research and write what you have learned about this pattern.

_____

_____

_____

Day 10: Pattern Awareness

Choose the pattern that seems least like you—research and write what you have learned.

_____

_____

_____

Day 11: Pattern Awareness

Randomly pick a pattern to research and make a list of all the people you know who fit that pattern.

_____

_____

_____

_____

Day 12: Pattern Awareness

Pick a pattern that irritates you and keep a running tab of how many people you are in contact with that fit that pattern.

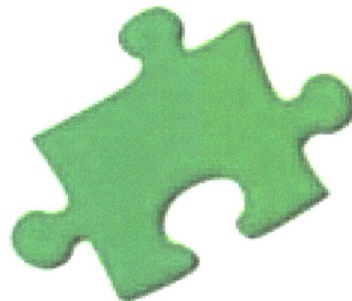

_____

_____

_____

_____

Day 13: Pattern Awareness

Pick a pattern and see how many times it shows up today—make a list of the phrases or words that fit the pattern.

_____

_____

_____

_____

Day 14: Pattern Awareness

Observe what triggers your primary pattern and write down 10 emotion words that fit into this pattern.

_____

_____

_____

_____

Day 15: Pattern Awareness

Observe who makes you angry and the first thoughts you have about the person.

_____

_____

_____

Observe all aspects of the situation and see if you can separate the person or the situation into categories.

_____

_____

_____

Day 16: Pattern Awareness

From the 8 patterns remaining on the list pick that one that is most like you and research.

_____

_____

_____

Day 17: Pattern Awareness

From the 7 patterns remaining pick the one you observe in your boss or supervisor and research.

_____

_____

_____

_____

_____

> *Let us not look back in anger or forward in fear, but around in awareness*
>
> *- James Thurber*

Day 18: Pattern Awareness

From the 6 remaining pick the one that causes you the most irritation and research.

_____

_____

_____

_____

_____

Day 19: Pattern Awareness

From the 5 remaining patterns, select the one that reminds you of one of your parents or caregivers and research it.

_____

_____

_____

_____

Day 20: Pattern Awareness

Do "**STOP**" exercise and notice your ways of handling your anger. **STOP** once an hour, for four hours and notice what has annoyed you or made you angry.

Hour One: _

Hour Two: _

Hour Three: _

Hour Four: _

Day 21: Pattern Awareness

From the 4 remaining patterns, pick the one that peeks your curiosity and research.

_____

_____

_____

_____

Day 22: Pattern Awareness

From the 3 remaining patterns pick one that fits best into following sentence:

When a _____ wants something from me, I want to run in the opposite direction.

Research the pattern.

_____

_____

_____

_____

_____

Thinking is the talking of the soul to itself. - Plato

Day 23: Pattern Awareness

From the 2 remaining patterns, research and write about someone you know who is the epitome of this pattern.

_____

_____

_____

_____

Day 24: Pattern Awareness

Notice the emotions this pattern represents for you.

Research.

_____

_____

_____

_____

_____

Day 25: Reflection

Take time today to enjoy your new learning and at end of the day write down one way you view yourself or others differently.

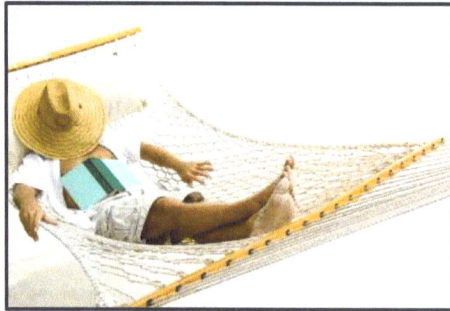

_____

_____

Day 26: Stress-O-Meter

Write down a recent situation that caused you stress.

_____

_____

_____

_____

On a 1 to 10 scale, rate the level for the above situation.

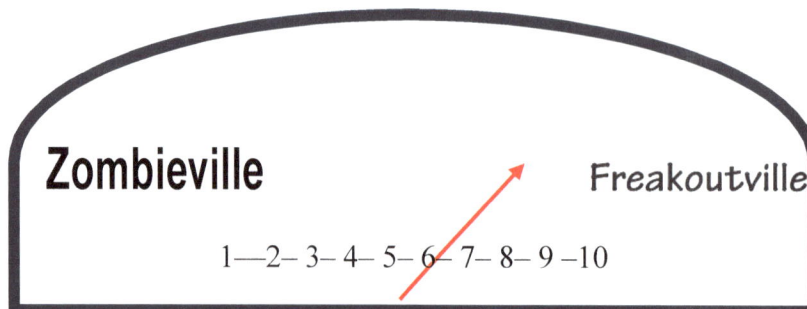

Zombieville   Freakoutville

1—2– 3– 4– 5– 6– 7– 8– 9 –10

Day 27: Patterns and Emotions

GLAD/SAD/MAD

Take each of the 13 patterns and put them in the column where you think they belong. There is no right or wrong answer. It's your opinion.

GLAD	SAD	MAD

Day 28: Glad

Take those in GLAD column and write down names of people who fit those patterns
—just notice!!

_____

_____

_____

_____

Day 29: Sad

Take those in SAD column and write down names of people who fit those patterns
— just notice!!

_____

_____

_____

_____

Day 30: Mad

Take those in MAD column and write down names of people who fit those patterns
—just notice!!

_____

_____

_____

_____

Take today and relax!!!

You have just completed the first part of your training!

Give yourself a gift of appreciation today!

The Way OUT

Observe

Understand

Transform

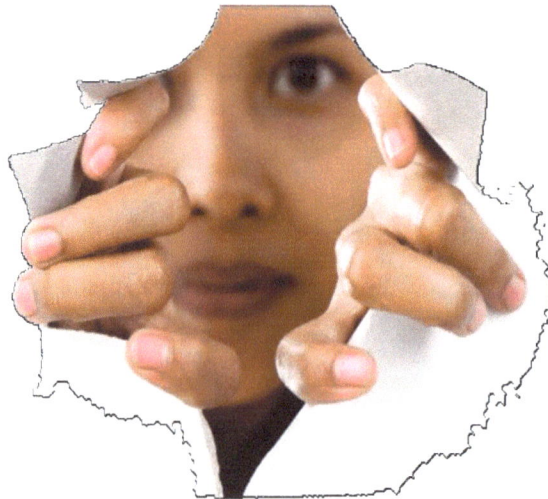

From NOW to NEW

Ready to UNDERSTAND

Understanding: *the awareness of the connection between individual pieces of information. Knowledge is the simple awareness of bits of information and understanding allows the knowledge to be put to use. When you understand, you see the patterns that connect.*

> "Everything that irritates us about others can lead us to
>
> an understanding of ourselves"
>
> Carl Gustav Jung

Day 31: Understand and Interact

This will help you see, hear, and appreciate relationships.

Tell one person one reason they mean something to you.

Write down how the conversation went.

_____

_____

_____

_____

_____

A clear understanding of negative emotions

dismisses them.

- Vernon Howard

Day 32: Understand and Interact

Tell one person today one reason they are upsetting you.

Write down how the conversation went.

_____

_____

_____

_____

_____

Day 33: Understand and Interact

Make a list of "change agent" words and from your list use one or two in meetings today. For example: a "change agent" word is a word that evokes bringing about transformation; such as inspire, motivate, and passion.

_____

_____

_____

_____

_____

I don't understand you. You don't understand me.
What else do we have in common?

- Ashleigh Brilliant

Day 34: Understand and Silence

When you find yourself becoming upset—choose silence and notice its impact on others.

Day 35: Understand and Memory

Take some magazines and find pictures that remind you of your past.
Note what makes you GLAD, SAD, and MAD.

_____

_____

_____

_____

_____

Day 36: Understand and Feel

Make a list of how you take care of others; (*i.e. run errands, buy gifts and goodies*).
Note how this makes you feel.

_____

_____

_____

_____

_____

> *The man of understanding finds everything laughable.*
>
> *-Johann Wolfgang Von Goethe*

Day 37: "NO" is a complete sentence.

Pick one thing from Day 36 list that annoys you. Decide to say "NO" and notice the reaction —just do **one thing** .

_____

_____

_____

_____

_____

_____

> *The power of intuitive understanding will protect you from harm until the end of your days.*
>
> *- Lao– Tza*

Day 38: Understand and Notice

Note the ways others help you. Notice how you feel in letting others help you or not.

_____

_____

_____

_____

_____

Day 39: Situation

Take time to write down a situation from the last few weeks that was particularly upsetting.
Look for the patterns that repeat. You will use this as an example for next 2 days.

_____

_____

_____

_____

_____

_____

> *If you want to understand today, you have to search yesterday.*
>
> *- Pearl S. Buck*

Day 40: Situation

Take the issue from Day 39 and spend 5-10 minutes in silence until you find a similar situation from the
past 5 or so years. Write it down.

_____

_____

_____

_____

_____

_____

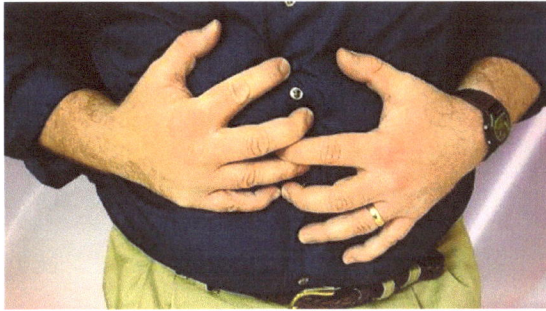

Day 41: Situation

Take the situation from Day 39 and do the following; put your hand on your stomach (gut) area and think back to earliest time when you had feelings similar to Day 39. Write it down.

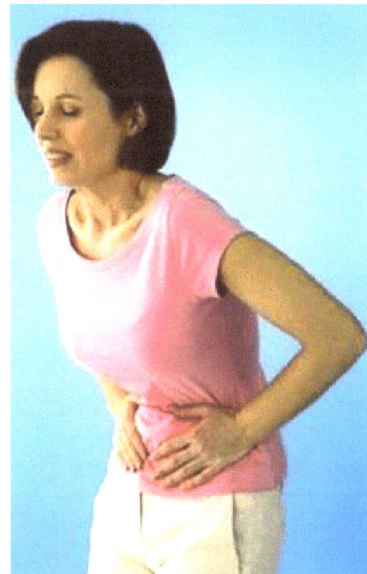

_____

_____

_____

_____

_____

_____

Day 42: Understand and Connect the Dots

Understand and connect the dots. Go back– way back to Day 9 and scan each page up to today.
Find patterns that connect and name them.

_____

_____

_____

_____

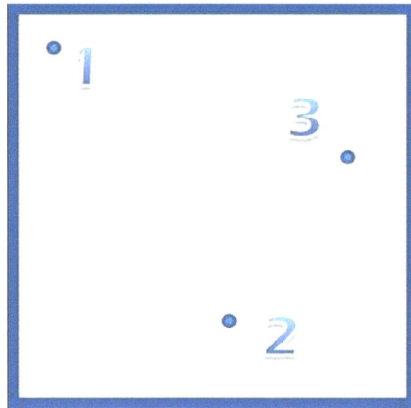

Day 43: Understand the Situation

From Day 39-42, write a short, short story with a new ending based upon what you have learned.

_____

_____

_____

_____

Values

Abundance	Commitment	Efficiency	Hygiene	Persistence	Silence
Acceptance	Compassion	Empathy	Imagination	Persuasiveness	Simplicity
Accessibility	Completion	Encouragement	Impact	Philanthropy	Solidarity
Accomplishment	Confidence	Endurance	Impartiality	Popularity	Stability
Acknowledgement	Connection	Energy	Independence	Power	Strength
Adaptability	Consciousness	Enjoyment	Insightfulness	Pragmatism	Structure
Adventure	Contribution	Enthusiasm	Inspiration	Presence	Success
Affection	Control	Excellent	Integrity	Privacy	Support
Ambition	Conviction	Expectancy	Intelligence	Proactivity	Sympathy
Amusement	Coolness	Experience	Intimacy	Professionalism	Synergy
Appreciation	Cooperation	Expertise	Intuition	Prosperity	Teamwork
Assertiveness	Correctness	Fairness	Investing	Punctuality	Thankfulness
Attentiveness	Courage	Fame	Joy	Realism	Thoughtfulness
Attractiveness	Courtesy	Family	Justice	Reason	Timeliness
Awareness	Creativity	Fashion	Kindness	Recognition	Traditionalism
Balance	Credibility	Fidelity	Knowledge	Relaxation	Tranquility
Beauty	Curiosity	Finance	Leadership	Reliability	Trust
Belonging	Decisiveness	Fitness	Learning	Religiousness	Truth
Benevolence	Decorum	Freedom	Liberty	Resilience	Understanding
Bravery	Dependability	Fun	Logic	Resolution	Uniqueness
Brilliance	Determination	Generosity	Longevity	Resolve	Unity
Calmness	Devotion	Giving	Love	Respect	Usefulness
Camaraderie	Dignity	Gratitude	Loyalty	Restraint	Vision
Candor	Direction	Growth	Mastery	Sacredness	Wealth
Care	Discipline	Guidance	Maturity	Satisfaction	Wisdom
Carefulness	Discovery	Happiness	Mindfulness	Security	Youthfulness
Celebrity	Discretion	Health	Motivation	Self-control	Zeal
Certainty	Diversity	Heart	Openness	Selflessness	
Challenge	Dominance	Helpfulness	Optimism	Sensitivity	
Charity	Drive	Heroism	Organization	Sensuality	
Chastity	Duty	Honesty	Originality	Serenity	
Cleanliness	Eagerness	Honor	Passion	Service	
Cleverness	Economy	Hospitality	Peace	Sexuality	
Closeness	Education	Humility	Perfection	Speed	
Comfort	Effectiveness	Humor	Pleasure	Spirit	

Day 44: Values

Make a list of your values. Keep list between 5-15 items.

_____

_____

_____

_____

_____

_____

_____

_____

Day 45: Values

Put values in order of preference. Take first 3 and write down where they came from—who were the guiding forces of your top 3 values.

1. _

2. _

3. _

> *Keep constantly in mind how many things you yourself have witnessed changes to already.*
> *The universe is change, life is understanding. - Marcus Aurelius*

Day 46: Inspire

Choose one of the people who inspired you. If alive ask them for their 3 key values.
Ask 'who' their guiding force was.

_____

_____

_____

_____

_____

_____

Day 47: Values Expressed

Note how you show the world what you value and how that is expressed.

_____

_____

_____

_____

_____

_____

> *Nobody can go back and start a new beginning, but anyone can start today and make a new ending.*
> *- Maria Robenson*

Day 48: Persecutor/Victim/Rescuer

Look at the following **P**ersecutor/**V**ictim/**R**escuer **(P/V/R)** model.
Where do you fit in the triangle?

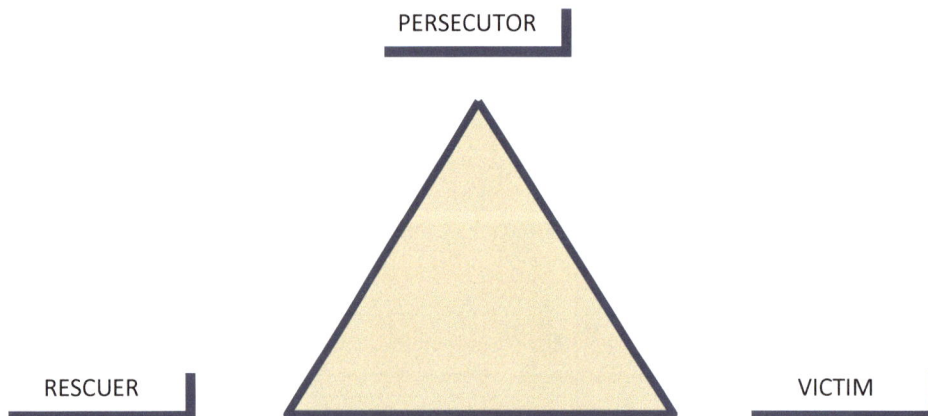

_____

_____

_____

_____

_____

_____

PERSECUTOR

RESCUER

VICTIM

Day 49: P/V/R

Answer questions

Where did you learn to take on the role of **P/V/R**?

_____

_____

_____

Who had these roles in your family as you grew up?

_____

_____

_____

Day 50: P/V/R

Answer questions

Take the **P/V/R** triangle into work. Name those who play the roles—where do you fit in?

_____

_____

_____

_____

_____

> *When I was nine, I had this girlfriend and we used to have running races in the park. I wanted to be like Superman and fly in and rescue her.*
>
> *- Orlando Bloom*

Day 389:

Listen to the stories of the people that you see as part of the **P/V/R** Triangle.
Ask one of them which pattern is their driving force—then <u>just listen</u>.

Day 52: Clarity

Paraphrase for clarity: say "what I hear you saying is…."

_____

_____

_____

_____

_____

_____

_____

Day 53: Be Empathic

Practice with a friend.

Say "I hear you"; do not change subject nor talk about yourself.

Restrain from giving advice. Write down how it felt.

_____

_____

_____

Day 54: Be Empathic

Practice with a colleague at work.

Say "I hear you"; do not change subject nor talk about yourself.

Restrain from giving advice. Write down how it felt.

_____

_____

_____

Day 55: Be Empathic

Practice with a family member.

Say "I hear you"; do not change subject nor talk about yourself.

Restrain from giving advice. Write down how it felt.

_____

_____

_____

Be who you are and say what you feel because those who mind don't matter and those who matter don't mind.
- Dr. Seuss

Day 56: Empathy and Interconnection

Take a situation where you were VERY upset. Write it down as if you were the other person —create a dialogue and say what you have learned.

_____

_____

_____

_____

_____

Day 57: Knowing Co-workers

List the 5 key people you work with. How much do you know about them?

Are they married/in a relationship?

_____

What are their skills?

_____

What are their challenges at work?

_____

What do they enjoy as hobbies?

_____

Where did they grow up?

_____

Day 58: Be Positive

Make it a point to greet everyone you meet today and make a short, positive comment.
Write down how it felt.

_____

_____

_____

_____

Day 59: Impact of Others

Call or send notes to at least 5 people who have impacted your life.

Write how it felt.

_____

_____

_____

_____

Day 60: Understand and Sharing

Share with 3 people close to you what you have learned about your patterns.

_____

_____

_____

MAKE A COMMITMENT TO DO MORE THAN:

Exist	⟶	Live
Touch	⟶	Feel
Hear	⟶	Listen
Listen	⟶	Understand
Look	⟶	Observe
Love	⟶	Serve
Think	⟶	Ponder
Talk	⟶	Say it meaningfully

You have just finished the second third of your training.

Take time alone, time with friend, loved ones; soak, swim…...

Take today to "go mindless"

With awareness and understanding comes the ability to act in a more responsible and caring way.

- Sylvia Lafair

The Way OUT

Observe

Understand

Transform

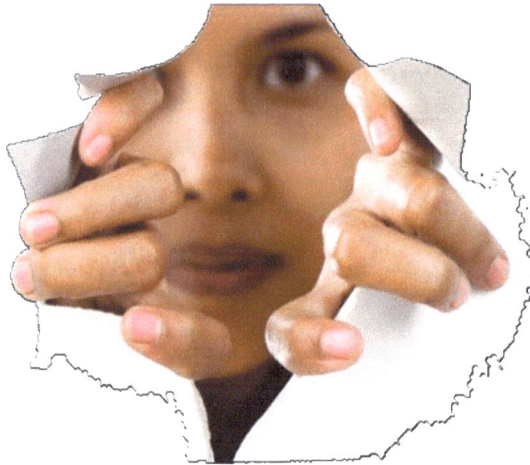

From NOW to NEW

TRANSFORM

Transform: *a change, often radical when one can no longer go back to the way things were. A change which alters the general character and make of life; germ into embryo, egg into the animal, child into adult.*

When we quit thinking primarily about ourselves and our own self - preservation, we undergo a truly heroic transformation of consciousness

- Joseph Campbell

Day 61: Assumptions

Check your assumptions.

Make sure what is expected of you at work is clear, if not, go to the proper person and ask.

Day 62: Patterns

Make a list of those you work closely with.

Name the primary pattern of each.

Name	Pattern

Day 63: Patterns

Take the first pattern: Super Achiever to Creative Collaborator. Find people you know in your history or in the media who have the transformed pattern of Creative Collaborator and jot down some thoughts about them.

_____

_____

_____

_____

_____

Day 64: Patterns

Research patterns: Rebel to Community Builder, Procrastination to Realizer, Clown to Humorist. Find people you respect and admire who have the healthy transformed patterns.

_____

_____

_____

_____

_____

> *Return to the root and you will find the meaning. - Sengston*

Day 65: Patterns

Research patterns: Persecutor to Visionary, Victim to Explorer, Rescuer to Mentor.

Find people you respect and admire who have the healthy transformed patterns.

_____

_____

_____

_____

_____

_____

Day 66: Patterns

Research patterns: Drama Queen/King to Story Teller, Martyr to Integrator, Pleaser to Truth Teller.

Find people you respect and admire who have the healthy transformed patterns.

_____

_____

_____

_____

_____

_____

Never apologize for showing feeling. When you do so, you apologize for the truth.

- Benjamin Disraeli

Day 67: Patterns

Research patterns: Avoider to Initiator, Denier to Trust Builder, Splitter to Peacemaker.

Find people you respect and admire who have the healthy transformed patterns.

_____

_____

_____

_____

_____

_____

Peptalk™ (Pattern Encounter Process)

Reference pages 157-167 in "Don't Bring It to Work" and page 62 of this guidebook.

You begin Peptalk™ by thinking about a pattern you wish to change, then letting your memory take you to a difficult or conflict-laden work situation where the pattern is pronounced.

Day 68: Peptalk

Pick a person/situation and practice Peptalk by writing it down or talking it into a recorder.

_____

_____

_____

_____

_____

_____

> *I believe in looking reality straight in the eye and denying it.*
>
> *- Garrison Keillor*

Day 69: Peptalk

Find a colleague and have them critique your Peptalk.

_____

_____

_____

_____

_____

_____

Day 70: Peptalk

Go to "the source" and complete the Peptalk process.

_____

_____

_____

_____

_____

_____

As human beings, our greatness is not so much in being able to remake the world—that is the myth of the atomic age—as is being able to remake ourselves.
- Gandhi

Day 71: Truth with Others

Fill in chart.

Put Person's Name	Where has trust been diminished?	What is truth you want to tell them?

Day 72: Truth Sentences

Practice truth sentences with individuals in Day 71 chart.

_____

_____

_____

> *The curious paradox is that when I accept myself just as I am, then I can transform.*
> *- Carl Rogers*

Day 73: Trust

Write down 3 people you trust and answer the following.

How do they respond to conflict?

_____

_____

_____

What do they offer you in the relationship?

_____

_____

_____

Day 74: Cautious

Write down 3 people you are cautious about and answer the following.

What makes you cautious?

_____

_____

_____

What can you say to make the relationship safer?

_____

_____

_____

Day 75: Rate Yourself

What part do you play in making your organization/team environment safe and trusting?
Rate yourself **(High, Medium, and Low)** on positivity and negativity.

_____

Day 76: Control

What happens when you are in control/not in control?

_____

_____

_____

_____

Day 77: Complaints

How do you make your complaints known to others?

_____

_____

_____

_____

Day 78: Collaborate

How do you collaborate?

Write down 3 ways you give feedback and how others respond.

_____

_____

_____

_____

_____

Day 79: Feedback

Write down 3 ways you receive feedback. How do you respond– do you accept, appreciate, acknowledge, defend, justify, attack? How do you ask others for feedback?

_____

_____

_____

_____

_____

_____

_____

Be creative– when you create you get a little endorphin rush. Why do you think Einstein looked like that?
-Robin Williams

Day 80: Delegate

How able are you to delegate? How do you hold the person accountable for the assignment?
How were jobs delegated to you? How did you know if you did a good job?

_____

_____

_____

_____

_____

Day 81: Rate Yourself

How do you respond to criticism? What is the risk if you are not right? Rate yourself. Do you need to be seen
as having all the answers and being in charge to make sure situations will be handled properly?

_____

_____

_____

_____

_____

Day 82: Rate Yourself

How do you rate yourself on inclusion/exclusion scale?
What can you do differently?

_____

_____

_____

_____

Day 83: Judging others

Write a few sentences describing how you judge others.

_____

_____

_____

_____

Day 84: Judging

Take a few minutes and think about a time you judged someone. Fill in the chart.

Person	Situation	Judgment

Day 85: Relationships

Write down 4 key relationships from childhood that supported high integrity/low integrity/mixed messages?

_____

_____

_____

What did you learn about yourself?

About others.

About relationships.

_____

_____

_____

_____

_____

Day 86: Patterns and Commitment

What are the 4 major patterns you are willing to transform?

Write a commitment sentence for each pattern.

_____

_____

_____

_____

_____

_____

Day 87: Patterns and Commitment

Make a list of behavior patterns you want to change and commit to check off (give yourself a star) on days you have "break-throughs".

_____

_____

_____

_____

Day 88: Sound Bites

Make a list of "sound bites" where you change language to transformed way of talking.

_____

_____

_____

_____

Day 89: Transformed

Write down how you have changed and what you still want to work on.

_____

_____

_____

_____

_____

If we have no peace, it is because we have forgotten that we belong to each other. —Mother Teresa

Day 90: Pattern Aware

Offer to mentor someone, for example, a new colleague, a college student, or youth in your community in becoming Pattern Aware.

What the caterpillar calls the end of the world, the

master calls a butterfly. - Anonymous

Live happily ever after...

- Do one extra act of kindness each week

- Take one extra risk (personal or professional each week)

- Take one extra hour just for yourself each week

- Give one extra thank you each week

- Turn one negative thought to a positive each week

13 Most Common Patterns
and Their Transformations

The **Super Achiever** – must win at all costs

Becomes the **Creative Collaborator** – sees the importance of team work and no one wins unless we all do

The **Rebel** – can't accept any authority

Becomes the **Community Builder** – pulls people together for positive change impacting the larger group

The **Procrastinator** – won't finish anything

Becomes the **Realizer** – a sense that all things are possible

The **Clown**– reduces everything to a joke

Becomes the **Humorist** – uses humor at the right moments, timing is everything

The **Persecutor** – bullies people into misery

Becomes the **Visionary** – masters of the art and craft of conflict transformation

The **Victim** – too scared to take any action

Becomes the **Explorer** – curious and adventurous, finding new ways to solve problems

The **Rescuer** – demands to be the big hero

Becomes the **Mentor** – listens and gives good advice at the right time

Continued on next page...

13 Most Common Patterns
and Their Transformations

Continued...

The **Drama Queen/King** – makes emotional scenes

Becomes the **Storyteller** – unites those around them to collaborate by use of a good story for motivation

The **Martyr** – does everyone else's work

Becomes the **Integrator** – brings people together to share the work load so no one feels over-burdened

The **Pleaser** – says what folks want to hear

Becomes the **Truth teller** – simply tells the truth without grandstanding or lecturing

The **Avoider** – dodges work and responsibility

Becomes the **Initiator** – steps up to handle conflict; no longer fears being judged

The **Denier** – won't face problems directly

Becomes the **Trust Builder** – faces all problems, asks lots of questions

The **Splitter** – secretly sets up conflict

Becomes the **Peacemaker** – works to preserve the integrity of the whole system, not one team over another—a win/win attitude

Peptalk™

Reference pages 157-167 in "Don't Bring It to Work"

You begin Peptalk (Pattern Encounter Process) by thinking about a pattern you wish to change, then letting your memory take you to a difficult or conflict-laden work situation where the pattern is pronounced.

Find a friend or several friends who would be willing to role-play with you, with you playing yourself. Give your helpers a full description of the other person, including physical characteristics, the person's job responsibilities, how the person communicates, and how the person tends to react emotionally.

SAMPLE Peptalk:

One of my clients was a CEO who needed to transform his troubled relationship with his CFO. The CEO scanned to find the pattern he wished to transform. Avoider came out loud and clear. The CEO hated to confront others and saw the CFO as a procrastinator who was always late with his financials. During the first five role play rehearsals of his Peptalk, the CEO failed to imagine a truly transformed encounter and wound up berating the CFO as a procrastinator, never claiming his own avoider pattern. This was to be expected– by continuing to talk about the other guy, he could avoid his own discomfort. On the sixth attempt, he finally turned it around, and this is what his initial approach sounded like:

> *"Elliot, you are a very competent CFO, and I trust the quality of your work. Yet, it is never done in a timely fashion and my tendency, as an avoider, is to shrug my shoulders and not say anything. The problem is that tension builds within me, and I find myself looking for reasons to stay away from you and send others to you to get the information I need. All this inhibits progress in the company, especially now that we are in acquisition mode. I want to change my avoider behavior to become an initiator. So, I'm not going away and I'm not sending others to do my bidding. I want to sit with you and develop a plan that will work for both of us."*

As the CEO finished the role play, he said, "Oh my God, I finally get it: Elliot is just like my stepfather. The man was a powerful force in my life and held the purse strings, yet I never felt I could talk with him directly, and I used to send my younger brothers to him when I needed money for something. Wow! Who would have thought that I avoid Elliot just like I did my stepfather?

By the time the CEO had his actual Peptalk with Elliot, it had lost the ragged edge of challenge. The conversation was not an unfinished dialogue between stepson and stepfather, but rather a polished and productive business exchange between CEO and CFO.

Sylvia Lafair, PhD, is President of Creative Energy Options, Inc. (CEO), a global consulting company that targets and transforms workplace patterns for success.

Dr. Lafair's programs and executive coaching impact individuals and teams to decrease conflict and increase productivity. Her award winning book, *'Don't Bring It to Work,'* (2009 Jossey-Bass), is listed as one of the top 20 books for emerging leaders. Lafair's research shows that, much as we like to believe that our behavior is entirely rational and governed by our conscious mind, our thoughts and actions are often driven by the roles we learned in our families as children. And under pressure, we tend to revert to old patterns, often creating workplace drama that diverts attention from the business and undermines productivity.

As a keynote speaker, workshop leader and webinar presenter, Sylvia engages audiences with her natural storytelling ability. She weaves her knowledge about personal relationships and business culture into easily understood messages, using both humor and suspense that leave audiences with information to take back to the office immediately put into practice.

Dr. Lafair has been quoted in **TIME, Fortune, Forbes, The New York Times** and **The Wall Street Journal** and among many radio and TV appearances, she has been a guest on the **TODAY Show** featuring her award winning book, *'GUTSY: How Women Leaders Make Change.'* Sylvia's newest book, *'UNIQUE: How Story Sparks Diversity, Inclusion, and Engagement'* just released, and is already on the hot list of "must reads" winning awards already.

As a noted authority on leadership, an award winning author, and executive coach, her message is unique and timely; her insights universal and relevant. Office drama and politics, human resource issues, absenteeism, and litigation often increase when stress is high in companies. This is where Dr. Lafair's unique model becomes vitally important as she teaches managers and teams how to transform ingrained patterns that get in the way of effective collaboration and organizational productivity.

Sylvia's Total Leadership Connections™ program has won awards in 2011, 2013 and is now listed among the top 12 programs for leadership in the country, by H.R.com/Leadership Excellence in 2014!

For more information please visit Sylvia on LinkedIn, Facebook, or send her a tweet on Twitter!

If you haven't already—take the Pattern Aware Quiz

at **www.sylvialafair.com** and **www.ceoptions.com**

Action is the antidote to despair. - Joan Baez

**Follow Us on Twitter… Like Us on Facebook…Watch Us on YouTube
Join Us on LinkedIn…Hang with Us on Google**

I'm Sylvia Lafair at

creative energy options

CEO

elevating leadership skills

Corporate Headquarters

45 Country Place Lane
White Haven, PA 18661
570.636.3858
info@ceoptions.com

www.ceoptions.com
www.sylvialafair.com
www.retreatpa.com

www.ingramcontent.com/pod-product-compliance
Lightning Source LLC
LaVergne TN
LVHW072106070426
835509LV00002B/41